Collins

Reading Comprehension Progress Tests

Year 3/P4

Author:
Josh Lury

Series editor:
Stephanie Austwick

William Collins's dream of knowledge for all began with the publication of his first book in 1819.

A self-educated mill worker, he not only enriched millions of lives, but also founded a flourishing publishing house. Today, staying true to this spirit, Collins books are packed with inspiration, innovation and practical expertise. They place you at the centre of a world of possibility and give you exactly what you need to explore it.

Collins. Freedom to teach.

Published by Collins
An imprint of HarperCollins*Publishers*
The News Building, 1 London Bridge Street, London, SE1 9GF, UK
1st Floor, Watermarque Building, Ringsend Road, Dublin 4, Ireland

> Browse the complete Collins catalogue at **www.collins.co.uk**

© HarperCollinsPublishers Limited 2019

10 9 8 7 6 5 4 3 2 1

ISBN 978-0-00-833344-7

All rights reserved. No part of this publication may be reproduced, stored in a retrieval system, or transmitted in any form by any means, electronic, mechanical, photocopying, recording or otherwise, without the prior written permission of the Publisher or a licence permitting restricted copying in the United Kingdom issued by the Copyright Licensing Agency Ltd, 5th Floor, Shackleton House, 4 Battle Bridge Lane, London, SE1 2HX.

British Library Cataloguing-in-Publication Data

A catalogue record for this publication is available from the British Library.

Author: Josh Lury
Series editor: Stephanie Austwick
Publisher: Katie Sergeant
Product Manager: Catherine Martin
Development editor: Judith Walters
Copyeditor and typesetter: Hugh Hillyard-Parker
Proofreader: Catherine Dakin
Cover designers: The Big Mountain
Production controller: Katharine Willard

The publishers gratefully acknowledge the permission granted to reproduce the copyright material in this book. Every effort has been made to trace copyright holders and to obtain their permission for the use of copyright material. The publishers will gladly receive any information enabling them to rectify any error or omission at the first opportunity.

TEXT

An extract on p.7 from *Mudpuddle Farm* reprinted by permission of HarperCollins Publishers Ltd © 1995 Michael Morpurgo; An extract on p.14 from *Spotlight on Brazil* by Charlotte Coleman-Smith reprinted by permission of HarperCollins Publishers Ltd © HarperCollins Publishers Ltd 2015; An extract on p.15 from *Class Six and the Very Big Rabbit* reprinted by permission of David Higham Associates www.davidhigham.co.uk on behalf of the author © 2005 Martin Waddell; An extract on pp.21-22 from *I Never Know How Poems Start* reprinted by permission of HarperCollins Publishers Ltd © 2012 Michael Rosen; An extract on pp.23-24 from *Fabulous Creatures – Are They Real?* Reprinted by permission of HarperCollins Publishers Ltd © 2005 Scoular Anderson; An extract on pp.32-33 from *Harry the Poisonous Centipede* reprinted by permission of HarperCollins Publishers Ltd © 1996 Lynne Reid Banks; An extract on pp.40-41 from *Monster and Chips* reprinted by permission of HarperCollins Publishers Ltd © David O'Connell 2013; An extract on pp.49-50 from *Caribbean Carnival* by Jillian Powell reprinted by permission of HarperCollins Publishers Ltd © HarperCollins Publishers Ltd 2016; An extract on p.51 from *The Story of Nian – a Folk Tale from China* reprinted by permission of HarperCollins Publishers Ltd © Dr Wee Bee Geok 2015.

IMAGES

p.7 Reprinted by permission of HarperCollins Publishers Ltd © Shoo Rayner 2017; p.8 Xenia L/Shutterstock; p.14t Illustration by Roger Stewart (Beehive Illustration) and Ann Paganuzzi reprinted by permission of HarperCollins Publishers Ltd © HarperCollins Publishers Ltd 2015; p.14b Illustration by Roger Stewart (Beehive Illustration) and Ann Paganuzzi reprinted by permission of HarperCollins Publishers Ltd © HarperCollins Publishers Ltd 2015; p.15 Reprinted by permission of HarperCollins Publishers Ltd © Tony Ross 2005; p.21 Illustration by Yuliya Somina reprinted by permission of HarperCollins Publishers Ltd © HarperCollins Publishers Ltd 2012; p.23 Reprinted by permission of HarperCollins Publishers Ltd © 2005 Scoular Anderson; p.24 Reprinted by permission of HarperCollins Publishers Ltd © 2005 Scoular Anderson; p.30t VectorPixelStar/Shutterstock; p.30b kirian/Shutterstock; p.31 Alexander_P/Shutterstock; p.32 Reprinted by permission of HarperCollins Publishers Ltd © 1996 Tony Ross; p.40 Reprinted by permission of HarperCollins Publishers Ltd ©2013 David O'Connell; p.42 © HarperCollins Publishers Ltd 2019; p.49 Pablo Scapinachi/Shutterstock; p.50 Luca Santilli/Shutterstock; p.50 John de la Bastide/Shutterstock; p.51 Reprinted by permission of HarperCollins Publishers Ltd © 2015 Turine Tran.

Contents

How to use this book — 4

Year 3 Curriculum map: Yearly overview — 6

Year 3/P4 Half Termly Tests

Autumn Half Term Test 1
- From *Mudpuddle Farm* by Michael Morpurgo (fiction) — 7
- Letter to parents and carers (non-fiction) — 8
- Answer booklet — 9

Autumn Half Term Test 2
- From *Spotlight on Brazil* by Charlotte Coleman-Smith (non-fiction) — 14
- From *Class Six and the Very Big Rabbit* by Martin Waddell (fiction) — 15
- Answer booklet — 16

Spring Half Term Test 1
- 'I Invented the Frisbee' from *I Never Know How Poems Start* by Michael Rosen (poetry) — 21
- From *Fabulous Creatures – Are They Real?* by Scoular Anderson (non-fiction) — 23
- Answer booklet — 25

Spring Half Term Test 2
- School Trip, Sam's diary (non-fiction) — 30
- From *Harry the Poisonous Centipede* by Lynne Reid Banks (fiction) — 32
- Answer booklet — 34

Summer Half Term Test 1
- From *Monster and Chips* by David O'Connell (fiction) — 40
- 'Hollow Legs' by Josh Lury (poetry) — 42
- Answer booklet — 44

Summer Half Term Test 2
- From *Caribbean Carnival* by Jillian Powell (non-fiction) — 49
- From *The Story of Nian: A Folk Tale from China* by Dr Wee Bee Geok (fiction) — 51
- Answer booklet — 52

Mark schemes — 57

Record sheet — 63

How to use this book

Introduction

Collins *Reading Comprehension Progress Tests* have been designed to give you a consistent whole-school approach to teaching and assessing reading comprehension. Each photocopiable book covers the required reading comprehension objectives from the 2014 Primary English National Curriculum. For teachers in Scotland, the books can offer guidance and structure that is not provided in the Curriculum for Excellence Experiences and Outcomes or Benchmarks.

As standalone tests, independent of any teaching and learning scheme, the Collins *Reading Comprehension Progress Tests* provide a structured way to assess progress in reading comprehension skills, to help you identify areas for development, and to provide evidence towards expectations for each year group.

Assessment of higher order reading skills

At the end of KS1 and KS2, children are assessed on their ability to demonstrate reading comprehension. This is done through national tests (SATs) accompanied by teacher assessment. Collins *Reading Comprehension Progress Tests* have been designed to provide children with opportunities to explore a range of texts, whilst building familiarity with the format, language and style of the SATs. Using the tests with your classes each half-term will offer you a snapshot of your pupils' progress throughout the year.

The tests draw on a wide range of text types, including a selection of original stories, poems and non-fiction material. The questions follow the style and format of SATs papers at a level appropriate to the year group, and the tests provide increasing challenge within each year group and across the school. Through regular use of the progress tests, children should develop and practise the necessary skills required to complete the national tests confidently and proficiently.

How to use this book

In this book, you will find six photocopiable half-termly tests. Each child will need a copy of the test. You will also find a Curriculum Map on page 6 indicating the aspects of the Content Domain covered in each test across the year group. These have been cross-referenced with the appropriate age-related statements from the National Curriculum.

The Year 3 tests demonstrate standard SATs-style questions and mirror the recognised KS2 format of whole texts followed by an answer booklet. Each test includes two contrasting texts. There is no set amount of time for completion of these tests, but a guide is to allow approximately one minute per mark. However, the length of texts increases in Tests 5 and 6 so it is important to develop children's reading stamina and fluency and teach them how to retrieve information quickly, efficiently and accurately.

To help you mark the tests, you will find mark schemes that include the number of marks to be awarded, model answers and a reference to the elements of the Content Domain covered by each question.

Test demand

The tests have been written to ensure smooth progression in children's reading comprehension within the book and across the rest of the books in the series. Each test builds on those before it so that children are guided towards the expectations of the SATs at the end of KS1 and KS2.

Year group	Test	Number of texts per test	Length of text per test	Number of marks per test
3	Autumn 1	2	200 words each or 400 words in total	20
3	Autumn 2	2	200 words each or 400 words in total	20
3	Spring 1	2	200 words each or 400 words in total	20
3	Spring 2	2	200 words each or 400 words in total	20
3	Summer 1	2	300 words each or 600 words in total	20
3	Summer 2	2	300 words each or 600 words in total	20

Performance thresholds

The table below provides guidance for assessing how children perform in the tests. Most children should achieve scores at or above the expected standard, with some children working at greater depth and exceeding expectations for their year group. Whilst these threshold bands do not represent standardised scores, as in the end of key stage SATs, they will give an indication of how children are performing against the expected standard for their year group.

Year group	Test	Working towards	Expected	Greater Depth
3	Autumn 1	10 marks or below	11–15 marks	16–20 marks
3	Autumn 2	10 marks or below	11–15 marks	16–20 marks
3	Spring 1	10 marks or below	11–15 marks	16–20 marks
3	Spring 2	10 marks or below	11–15 marks	16–20 marks
3	Summer 1	10 marks or below	11–15 marks	16–20 marks
3	Summer 2	10 marks or below	11–15 marks	16–20 marks

Tracking progress

A record sheet is provided to help you illustrate to children the areas in which their reading comprehension is strong and where they need to develop. A spreadsheet tracker is also provided via **collins.co.uk/assessment/downloads** which enables you to identify whole-class patterns of attainment. This can be used to inform your next teaching and learning steps.

Editable download

All the files are available in Word and PDF format. Go to **collins.co.uk/assessment/downloads** to find instructions on how to download. The files are password protected and the password clue is included on the website. You will need to use the clue to locate the password in your book.

You can use these editable files to help you meet the specific needs of your class, whether that be by increasing or decreasing the challenge, by reducing the amount of questions, by providing more space for answers or increasing the size of text as required for specific children.

Year 3 Curriculum map: Yearly overview

National Curriculum objective (Year 3)	Content domain	Test 1 Fiction	Test 1 Non-fiction	Test 2 Non-fiction	Test 2 Fiction	Test 3 Poetry	Test 3 Non-fiction	Test 4 Non-fiction	Test 4 Fiction	Test 5 Fiction	Test 5 Poetry	Test 6 Non-fiction	Test 6 Fiction
Comment on words and phrases that capture the reader's interest and imagination.	2g Identify/explain how meaning is enhanced through choice of words and phrases.	●									●		●
Recognise some features of different forms of poetry.	n/a										●		
Explain the meaning of words in context.	2a Give / explain the meaning of words in context.	●	●	●	●	●	●	●	●	●	●	●	●
Draw inferences such as inferring characters' feelings, thoughts and motives from their actions, and justifying inferences with evidence.	2d Make inferences from the text / explain and justify inferences with evidence from the text.	●			●	●			●	●			●
Predict what might happen from details stated and implied.	2e Predict what might happen from details stated and implied.	●								●			●
Identify main ideas drawn from more than one paragraph (or verse) and summarise these.	2c Summarise main ideas from more than one paragraph.	●	●	●		●	●	●	●		●	●	●
Identify how language, structure and presentation contribute to meaning.	2g Identify/explain how meaning is enhanced through choice of words and phrases.	●	●	●	●	●	●	●	●	●	●	●	●
Retrieve and record information/identify key details from fiction and non-fiction texts.	2b Retrieve and record information / identify key details from fiction and non-fiction.	●	●	●	●	●	●	●	●	●	●	●	●

© HarperCollins*Publishers* Ltd 2019

From *Mudpuddle Farm*

by Michael Morpurgo

Old Thunder sailed majestically out through the gate and into the corn field beyond, his great cutters turning like the wheels of a giant paddle steamer.

"One man went to mow, went to mow a meadow," sang old Farmer Rafferty in his crusty, croaky kind of voice.

And behind him, Jigger, the usually sensible sheepdog, slunk through the gate and lay down in the cut corn, his nose on the ground in between his paws.

He smelt something, and what he smelt pleased him.

With the gate safely shut and Old Thunder roaring round the field, the animals at last crept out of their hiding places and stood watching by the gate – all except Mossop, who had fallen asleep in his drain.

"What's Jigger up to?" asked Diana the silly sheep, who always asked questions but never knew any answers.

Round and round the field went Old Thunder, churning out the straw behind him in long and golden rows. Round and round the field went Jigger, slinking low to the ground. And every now and then he would stop and stare at the square of standing corn, and every time he stopped, the square was a little bit smaller.

READWELL SCHOOL

18th July

Dear parents and carers,

It has come to my attention that there is a new craze among the pupils. I am writing to ask you to support me in making sure the situation does not get out of hand.

The children have been collecting a range of cards called Pyramids, which they use to build towers by stacking the cards together. The results certainly do look impressive, and to begin with I was happy with this as a playtime activity.

However, some of the pupils have become so skilled that the towers are now somewhat dangerous. For example, Anya constructed a replica of the Eiffel Tower which stood over a metre tall. I was very impressed until I discovered that it was strong enough for the children to climb and jump off. This kind of behaviour will only lead to injury, I am afraid.

Furthermore, the whole of Class 3B joined forces to create a structure resembling a fortress. The whole thing had a defensive wall, a solid door and no way in or out. It took Mr Shepherd and me 20 minutes to retrieve the children and return them to their lessons.

Now, while I am happy to see the pupils develop their engineering skills, I am less than happy to find that they are doing so at the expense of learning their spellings and times tables. I ask that all families restrict their children to 10 cards each and do not allow them to build anything that prevents the teachers from doing their jobs.

Yours in hope,

Ms Brunel

Year 3: Autumn Test 1 – Answer booklet

Name: Class: Date:

Questions 1–8 are about *Mudpuddle Farm* (page 7).

1 What is the name of the sheepdog?

_____

1 mark

2 Name **two** animals from the text.

✓ Tick **two**.

Old Thunder ☐

Diana ☐

Rafferty ☐

Mossop ☐

1 mark

3 Find evidence in the text to show why the sheep is *silly*.

_____

_____

_____

1 mark

4 Read the description of the farmer's singing.

Tick the **best option** to complete the sentence.

The farmer is _____ .

✓ Tick **one**.

angry ☐   old ☐   worried ☐

1 mark

© HarperCollins*Publishers* Ltd 2019

Year 3: Autumn Test 1 – Answer booklet

5 Number the sentences below from **1** to **4** to show the order in which they happen.

The first has been done for you.

The dog noticed a smell.	☐
Diana wondered about Jigger's behaviour.	☐
Old Thunder entered the field.	1
The animals slowly appeared from hiding.	☐

1 mark

6 Tick the option that **best predicts** why Jigger is interested in the *square of standing corn*.

✓ Tick **one**.

He likes the smell of cut grass.	☐
Another creature is hiding in the field.	☐
Diana has tricked him.	☐
Mossop is asleep in the field.	☐

1 mark

7 The sheepdog *slunk through the gate*.

What does the word *slunk* tell us about the way the sheepdog moved?

_____

_____

_____

2 marks

© HarperCollins*Publishers* Ltd 2019

Year 3: Autumn Test 1 – Answer booklet

8 Give **two** reasons why some of the animals might be afraid of Old Thunder.

1. _____

_____

2. _____

_____

2 marks

Questions 9–15 are about **'Letter to parents and carers'** (page 8).

9 Read the paragraph beginning:

However, some of the pupils

Find and **copy two** words that show Ms Brunel is concerned about safety.

1. _____

2. _____

1 mark

10 Describe how Ms Brunel's opinion of the cards has changed over time.

_____

_____

_____

2 marks

© HarperCollins*Publishers* Ltd 2019

11 Draw **three** lines to match the people to their activity.

Anya		constructed a building like a castle
Mr Shepherd		built a tower
Class 3B		tried to get children back into class

1 mark

12 Ms Brunel signs the letter *Yours in hope*.

Put ticks (✓) in the table to show which of these are **true** and which are **false**.

Sentence	True	False
She hopes the children get better at building.		
She hopes that parents and carers will support her.		
She is writing to someone called Hope.		

1 mark

13 The activity is described as *somewhat dangerous*.

Tick the option that **best matches** the meaning of the word *somewhat* in this sentence.

✓ Tick **one**.

a few ☐   very ☐   hardly ☐

1 mark

14 Give **two** ways that Anya's tower is impressive.

1. _____

   _____

2. _____

   _____

2 marks

15 **Find** these words in the text and draw **four** lines to match them to their correct meaning.

| results | | to find and bring back |

| replica | | stops or blocks |

| retrieve | | the final outcome |

| prevents | | an exact copy |

2 marks

From *Spotlight on Brazil*

by Charlotte Coleman-Smith

Groups of native Indians have lived in Brazil for thousands of years, but Pedro Álvares Cabral, a Portuguese explorer and nobleman, was the first person from Europe to reach Brazil. He arrived on 22 April 1500, on his way to India. After 1530, more people from Portugal and the rest of Europe followed him and settled in Brazil. As more and more Portuguese came to live in Brazil, Portuguese eventually became the official language.

Settlers and slaves

The early settlers realised that the fertile land was just right for growing sugar cane. Sugar soon **became** the most important crop in Brazil and made many landowners very rich. The landowners didn't have enough local workers, so they brought over people from West Africa as slaves and forced them to work on the sugar plantations.

Between 1550 and 1850, about five and a half million slaves were brought to Brazil in ships. They were squashed together in appalling conditions. Around 660,000 died before they even got to Brazil. The slave ships were known as "*tumbeiros*" (coffin carriers). Once in Brazil, slaves were poorly treated, and many didn't live beyond 30. Slavery was eventually abolished in 1888.

From *Class Six and the Very Big Rabbit*

by Martin Waddell

Class Six liked their teacher, Miss Bennett. She could do magic, like no one else could. She could wiggle her ears and make things disappear. Then she'd earwiggle again, and make them come back.

One day she did something different. She was reading Class Six a book about rabbits.

"Rabbits *are* nice," Miss Bennett said. Then she grinned and earwiggled. "I wish I was a rabbit!" she said.

And … there was a **fizzzz** …

And a **flash** …

And a **bang** …

… and Miss Bennett changed into a very big rabbit.

Class Six sat and looked at the very big rabbit and the very big rabbit sat looking right back at Class Six.

She was Miss Bennett-sized, and she had glasses like Miss Bennett. She was holding the book Miss Bennett had been reading, so Class Six knew it had to be her. They just didn't know how she had managed the trick.

Everyone cheered the big rabbit.

The big rabbit went back to the rabbit book and started reading again. At least she tried to read, but all that came out were squeaks.

"Rabbits can't read," Ranjit whispered to Rachel.

"You can't blame her for trying," Rachel whispered back.

Questions 1–7 are about **Spotlight on Brazil** (page 14).

1 When did the first European travel to Brazil?

_____

1 mark

2 Who made Portuguese the official language of Brazil?

✓ Tick **one**.

native Indians ☐

slaves from West Africa ☐

European settlers ☐

1 mark

3 Draw **four** lines to match each word from the text with its correct meaning.

appalling	good for growing
abolished	terrible
fertile	made a home
settled	stopped

1 mark

Year 3: Autumn Test 2 – Answer booklet

4 Number the sentences below from **1** to **4** to show the order in which they happened.

The first has been done for you.

Cabral first visited Brazil.	☐
Slaves were transported from Africa.	☐
Landowners discovered the land was fertile.	☐
Native Indians lived in Brazil for thousands of years.	1

1 mark

5 Give **two** reasons from the text that prove *slaves were poorly treated*.

1. _____

   _____

2. _____

   _____

2 marks

6 Read the paragraph beginning *The early settlers*.

Find and **copy** the word that means the same as 'wealthy'.

_____

1 mark

© HarperCollins*Publishers* Ltd 2019   17

7 Put ticks (✓) in the table to show which of these are **true** and which are **false**.

	True	False
Slaves were asked to make coffins.		
Pedro Álvares Cabral was travelling to India when he found Brazil.		
Landowners and slaves became very rich.		

2 marks

> Questions 8–15 are about *Class Six and the Very Big Rabbit* (page 15).

8 How did Miss Bennett perform magic?

_____

1 mark

9 What gave Miss Bennett the idea to turn into a rabbit?

_____

_____

1 mark

10 Give **two** ways that the class knew the rabbit was really Miss Bennett.

1. _____

   _____

2. _____

   _____

2 marks

11 Choose **one** option to complete the sentence in a way that matches the story.

✓ Tick **one**.

Ranjit and Rachel whispered because they _____

were afraid of the rabbit. ☐

didn't want to hurt her feelings. ☐

wanted to hear her read some more. ☐

1 mark

12 How do you think the class felt when Miss Bennett changed into a rabbit?

Support your answer with evidence from the text.

_____

_____

_____

2 marks

13 **Find** and **copy one** of the similarities between the rabbit and Miss Bennett.

_____

1 mark

14 Put ticks (✓) to show which sentences are **true** and which are **false**.

	True	False
The class had seen Miss Bennett turn into a rabbit before.		
Rachel was angry that Miss Bennett could not finish her story.		
The rabbit remained calm after the trick.		

2 marks

15 And… there was a *fizzzz* …

And a *flash* …

And a *bang* …

This is the moment when the magic happens.

What effect do you think the author is trying to create?

✓ Tick **one**.

sadness ☐

anger ☐

surprise ☐

1 mark

I Invented the Frisbee

from *I Never Know How Poems Start*

by Michael Rosen

On a camping trip
my brother and me
invented the Frisbee.

Frisbees that spin as they fly
as they zoom, as they dip.
A Frisbee:
it's a disc, a satellite,
a UFO, a spaceship.

The Frisbee –
that looks like it should hum
or whirr or buzz.
It doesn't even whisper.
It flies or spins.
That's what it does.

On a camping trip
my brother and me
invented the Frisbee.
I was seven.
My brother was 11.

We were washing the dishes –
thin, lightweight picnic plates.
My brother and me got bored.
It was getting late.

So we started throwing plates
that spin as they fly,
as they zoom, as they dip.
Look! That plate is
a disc, a satellite,
a UFO, a spaceship.
A plate
that looks like it should hum
or whirr or buzz.
It doesn't even whisper.
It flies and spins.
That's what it does.

No one knows
my brother and me
invented the Frisbee
on a camping trip
in 1953 …
… because we didn't
ever tell anyone
we did.

From *Fabulous Creatures – Are They Real?*
by Scoular Anderson

Fabulous creatures are those you read about in stories, especially in myths and legends. Some of these creatures really exist. Others don't. Do you know which in this book are real, and which are not?

Cerberus

Cerberus is a very unusual type of dog. He has three heads, and spines along his back like a dragon.

He's a fierce guard dog but can be quite friendly if you offer him bits of cake soaked in honey.

Is this fabulous creature real or not?

Cerberus is a three-headed dog in an ancient Greek legend. He was the guardian of Hades – the underworld where the spirits of people went when they died.

The spirits offered the dog bits of sweet cake to let them pass into Hades.

Coelacanth

A coelacanth is a huge, blue fish with powerful jaws and sharp teeth. Its body is covered in heavy, armoured scales and it has four thick fins at each corner of its body which allow it to walk.

Is this fabulous creature real or not?

The coelacanth lives in the Indian Ocean and the only walking it does is under water. Before 1938, scientists had found many rock fossils of coelacanths, but nobody had ever seen a live one. Everyone thought the fish had died out.

That changed when some South African fishermen found a strange fish in their nets – a coelacanth!

| Name: | Class: | Date: |

> Questions 1–8 are about '**I Invented the Frisbee**'
> (pages 21–22).

1 Which option best describes when the poet *Invented the Frisbee*?

✓ Tick **one**.

The brothers invented the frisbee _____ .

at school ☐   on holiday ☐   in the kitchen ☐

1 mark

2 Read the verse beginning *We were washing the dishes.*

Find and **copy two** words that show the plates were easy to throw

_____   _____

1 mark

3 Why did the boys begin throwing the plates?

_____

1 mark

4 Read the second verse. **Find** and **copy three** words the poet uses to describe how Frisbees move.

_____

_____

_____

1 mark

5 Put ticks (✓) in the table to show which statements are **true** and which are **false**.

Sentence	True	False
Frisbees and plates buzz and whirr.		
Frisbees don't make a sound as they fly.		
They whispered as they threw the plates.		

1 mark

6 Which word does the poet use to rhyme with *buzz*?

✓ Tick **one**.

hum ☐

fuzz ☐

does ☐

1 mark

7 The poet says *we didn't ever tell anyone*.

Put ticks (✓) to show whether each sentence is more likely to be **true** or **false**, based on the poem.

Sentence	True	False
They didn't know anyone to tell about it.		
They were worried they would get into trouble.		
They forgot all about it.		
They knew it was wrong to throw plates.		

2 marks

8 The poet says the Frisbee is *a spaceship*.

✓ Tick **one**.

This shows the poet's feelings of _____ .

excitement ☐

uncertainty ☐

boredom ☐

1 mark

Questions 9–15 are about *Fabulous Creatures – Are They Real?* (pages 23–24).

9 Put ticks (✓) in the table to show which of these are **true** and which are **false**.

	True	False
None of the creatures in the book exist.		
Myths and legends are types of stories.		
Fabulous creatures are from myths but not legends.		

1 mark

10 How can you make Cerberus more peaceful?

_____

_____

1 mark

11 Cerberus is described as *very unusual*. Find **two** pieces of evidence from the text that support this idea.

1. _____

2. _____

2 marks

12 Why is the word *fabulous* a suitable word to describe these creatures?

_____

_____

_____

2 marks

13 Read the description of the coelacanth. Draw **four** lines to match each body part to the appropriate description.

fins	strong
scales	heavy
jaws	sharp
teeth	thick

1 mark

14 Give **two** different pieces of evidence that the coelacanth is real.

1. _____

_____

2. _____

_____

2 marks

15 Can the coelacanth truly walk?

Explain your answer fully.

_____

_____

_____

_____

2 marks

School Trip – Sam's Diary

Thursday

Miss Singh said it was only a short journey, but the coach trip felt like for…ev…er. I sat next to Faye, which was great, but then she felt sick and moved to the front, so I was on my own.

When we arrived, everyone was so excited. I am sharing a bunk with Bella. The only problem is she can't decide whether to have the top or the bottom bed. I don't mind which one she chooses, but I do mind having to swap over our sleeping bags every five minutes. Well. Better go now – the bell just rang for dinner. I hope it's not pizza.

Yuck! It was, but I don't mind because we had a talent show and we came second. Billy won, like he always does. I knew he could juggle, but I didn't know he could do a handstand for over a minute!

Friday

We went to the castle and climbed right to the top of the tower, and Billy got in huge trouble. He tried to climb the portcullis and pretended he was an invading army.

We did laugh but I knew it was going to be BIG TROUBLE so I went to look at the suits of armour.

The room was long and full of weapons and chainmail. There was one sword called a broadsword. A kind lady said "Do you want to try and lift it?" and I nodded. I couldn't even lift it above my knee.

But then Miss S saw me and thought I was trying to steal it or something. Lucky that the lady said she was a curator, which means she looks after all the artefacts, and got me out of bother, or I'd have been going home early like someone else we know!

From *Harry the Poisonous Centipede*

by Lynne Reid Banks

Harry was a poisonous centipede.

You may think that's not a very nice thing to be. But Harry thought it was fine. He'd never been anything else, and he liked being what he was.

If you'd told him centipedes are nasty scary creepy-crawlies, he would have been very surprised and rather hurt.

And if you'd told him that biting things with poisonous pincers was wrong or cruel, he would probably have told you not to be ridiculous. How else would he get anything to eat, or defend himself from creatures wanting to eat him?

Of course, you couldn't have talked to Harry like that, even if you'd met him, because he couldn't have understood you. Harry could only speak to other centipedes in Centipedish. In fact, his real name wasn't Harry at all. It was (as nearly as I can write it) Hxzltl.

Hxzltl?

Yes. You see the problem at once. There are no vowel-sounds in Centipedish, just a sort of very faint crackling. What you could do is put in some vowel-sounds – some a's, e's, i's, o's and u's – so that you can try to say his real name. Then you could call him Hixzalittle. Or Hoxzalottle. Or perhaps even Haxzaluttle. But still you wouldn't be anywhere near the real sound of his name.

Which is why I call him Harry.

He lived in a very hot country – what we call the Tropics – with his mother.

Now, please don't start asking what her name was. Oh no. Please. Oh ... All right. Here goes. It was Bkvlbbchk. Bikvilababchuk? Bokvaliboobchak? Bakvolobibchawk? I don't know. Why bother? We'll never get it right.
Let's call her Belinda.

Belinda was also, of course, a poisonous centipede. A very large one – a good eight inches long, or twenty centimetres, if you want to be metric about it. Just imagine, eight inches of shiny, black, swift-moving centipede – a twenty-centi-centipede! Her body was something like a caterpillar's, in segments, but covered with hard, shiny, dark stuff – a sort of suit of armour, which is called a cuticle.

Year 3: Spring Test 2 – Answer booklet

| Name: | Class: | Date: |

Questions 1–8 are about School Trip – Sam's Diary (pages 30–31).

1 Sam wrote *the coach trip felt like for…ev…er*.

Which best explains why 'forever' is written like this?

✓ Tick **one**.

Sam forgot how to spell 'forever'. ☐

To make it like a puzzle. ☐

To show how it felt like a long time. ☐

Sam wanted to fill up more space. ☐

1 mark

2 Explain why Sam used the word *Yuck!*

_____

1 mark

3 Put ticks (✓) in the table to show which of these are **true** and which are **false**.

	True	False
Sam enjoyed sitting next to Faye.		
Faye moved after she had been sick.		
Sam hadn't really wanted to sit next to Faye.		

2 marks

4 What did Bella do to annoy Sam?

_____

_____

_____

1 mark

5 Choose **one** option that fills the gap.

✓ Tick **one**.

It was the first time they saw Billy _____ for over a minute.

juggle ☐   eat pizza ☐   do a handstand ☐

1 mark

6 Draw **four** lines to match each word on the left with its correct meaning.

portcullis	a weapon
artefact	someone who works at a museum
broadsword	an ancient or important object
curator	a defensive gate

2 marks

7 **Find** the sentence including the words *like someone else we know!*

Put ticks (✓) in the table to show which of these are **true** and which are **false**.

	True	False
Sam was told off by the curator.		
Billy had been sent home.		
The curator explained to the teacher to help Sam.		
The curator thought Sam was lucky to not go home.		

1 mark

8 Number the sentences below from **1** to **4** to show the order in which they happen.

dinner ☐

talent contest ☐

the trip to the castle ☐

discussion about where to sleep ☐

1 mark

Questions 9–15 are about *Harry the Poisonous Centipede* (pages 32–33).

9 **Find** and **copy two** words that show how Harry would feel if someone called him *scary*.

_____   _____

1 mark

10 What **two** reasons might Harry use to explain why he used his poisoned pincers.

✓ Tick **two**.

to prevent another creature harming him ☐

to climb walls and trees ☐

to stay cool in the heat ☐

to catch food to eat ☐

1 mark

11 The narrator says *he would probably have told you not to be ridiculous*.

✓ Tick **one** word that could replace *ridiculous*.

surprised ☐   silly ☐   names ☐

1 mark

12 Put ticks (✓) in the table to show which of these are **true** and which are **false**.

	True	False
Harry's friend is called Belinda.		
Belinda is Harry's mother.		
Belinda lives in a hot climate.		
Harry lives in a different country to Belinda.		

2 marks

13 Explain why the narrator calls him Harry instead of his real name.

_____

_____

_____

_____

2 marks

14 Find evidence from the text to:

a) describe how Belinda's body is like a caterpillar's body.

_____

_____

b) describe how Belinda's body is different from a caterpillar's body.

_____

_____

2 marks

15 Choose **one** option that best explains Harry's opinion of being a centipede.

Harry was happy being a centipede. ☐

Harry felt ashamed of being a centipede. ☐

Find and **copy** a phrase that supports your answer.

_____

_____

1 mark

From *Monster and Chips*
by David O'Connell

Joe had been sent on a perilous quest – to get chips for dinner. Mum had given him some magic tokens, or "money", as she liked to call it, and ordered him to find the finest chips in the land or die in the process. Now Joe the Fearless faced the stronghold of McGreasy's takeaway, the treasure of golden fried potato almost within his grasp. But alas! What monstrous horror blocked our hero's path?

"Oh look, it's that squirming little bum-toot, Joe Shoe!" sneered Grotty Grace, the school bully, snapping Joe out of his heroic daydream.

Grotty Grace was one of McGreasy's best customers, and had the body to prove it. Even a fire-breathing dragon with fearsome teeth and mighty jaws would have had trouble digesting Grotty Grace. She was standing in front of the takeaway door, munching messily on a McGreasy burger with extra everything.

Joe attempted to slide past her, but Grotty Grace pressed her spotty face up close so that her smelly burger-breath swept up his nose and poked his brain like stinky fingers.

"Let me get past, Grace!" said Joe. "I'm fetching some chips for my mum."

He tried to sound like Joe the Fearless, but with his nose screwed up he sounded more like a posh duck.

Grotty Grace laughed, her chins wobbling like angry jelly.

"Say that you're nothing but a squirming little bum-toot and I'll let you pass," said Grace, with a menacing growl. "And if you let me have some of your chips I might not thump you."

Joe needed a plan. He didn't want to get thumped but he wasn't going to give Grace any of his chips. He had to get her away from the door to the takeaway!

Hollow Legs

by Josh Lury

Where does he put it all?
My grandma used to say.
You must have hollow legs
To put all that away.

But she never did guess.
She never knew the half of it.
My stomach really is
A truly bottomless pit.

The entrance to the cave
Has sharp and jagged rocks
That crash and clash together
With grinding, slicing chomps.

Past the great white stones
A blind monster slurps and slides
Pushing the morsel further back
Until it drops inside.

Then … wait …
A final squash and squeeze
A squelching, gurgling gulp
And now it's flying free –

Down, down, into the dark
Into the empty abyss and further down
A never-ending free-fall
Into the great unknown.

Oh it echoes, echoes
As the chunks tumble, tumble.
The further it goes, goes
The louder the rumble, rumble.

The walls are covered in green slime
Digestive acids, bacteria,
Unwanted broccoli spears
Trapped in the interior.

Every bite and crumb and chunk
Adds to the grumble and roar
And nothing ever reaches
The cavern's infinite floor.

So that's where it all goes
If anyone ever asks.
I don't just have hollow legs
… They're only just the start.

Year 3: Summer Test 1 – Answer booklet

Name: Class: Date:

Questions 1–8 are about *Monster and Chips* (pages 40–41).

1 Read the first paragraph. Draw **four** lines to match Joe's daydream descriptions with their real meanings.

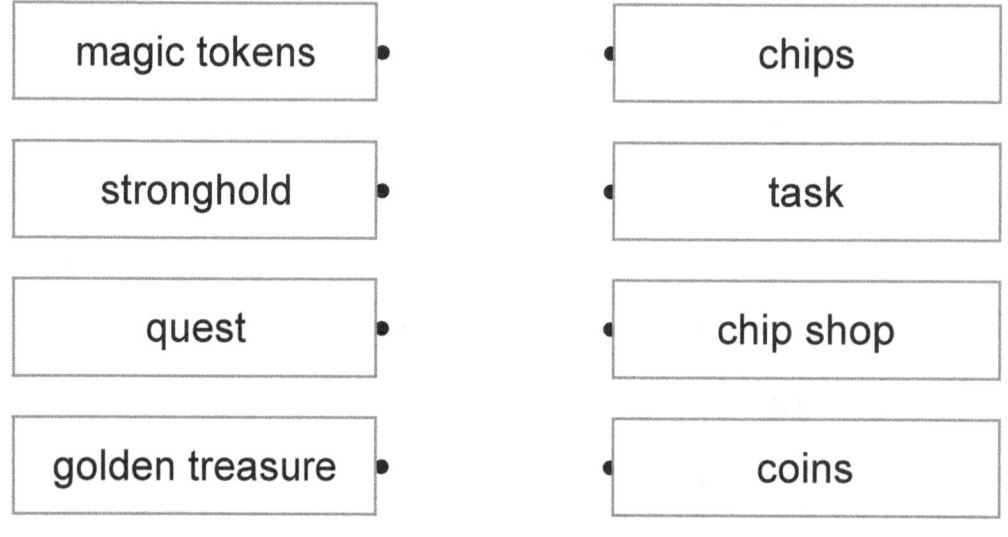

1 mark

2 Read the first paragraph. **Find** and **copy** a word that means the same as 'dangerous'.

_____

1 mark

3 The author writes that Grace *sneered*.

What does this tell us about her?

_____

_____

1 mark

© HarperCollins*Publishers* Ltd 2019

4 Put ticks (✓) in the table to show which of these are **true** and which are **false**.

	True	False
A dragon tried to eat Grace.		
Eating jelly made Grace angry.		
Joe was a type of duck.		

1 mark

5 Find the word *menacing* on page 41.

Which of the following words have a similar meaning?

✓ Tick **two**.

threatening ☐

quiet ☐

fierce ☐

hungry ☐

1 mark

6 When Joe tried to sound brave, he ended up sounding like a posh duck.

Why did Joe have *his nose screwed up*?

_____

1 mark

Year 3: Summer Test 1 – Answer booklet

7 Find **two** pieces of evidence that show Joe thinks he is like a knight on an adventure.

1. _____

_____

2. _____

_____

2 marks

8 Do you think Joe is going to give in to the bully?

Use information from the text to explain what you think might happen next.

_____

_____

_____

_____

2 marks

Questions 9–15 are about '**Hollow Legs**' (pages 42–43).

---

9 The poet describes *great white stones*.

✓ Tick **one** option to complete the sentence.

The stones represent _____ .

mountains ☐   teeth ☐   a monster ☐

1 mark

10 The poet uses the word *morsel*.

This means a very small piece of food. **Find** and **copy two** other words from the poem that have a similar meaning.

_____   _____

1 mark

11 What is the poet's opinion of broccoli?

Explain how you can tell.

_____

_____

1 mark

12 **Find** these words that are used in the poem:

squelching, gurgling, grumble, roar

Which sense do these words appeal to?

✓ Tick **one**.

sight ☐
taste ☐
hearing ☐
touch ☐

1 mark

13 The poet uses the word *abyss*. **Find** this word in the text.

What do you think *abyss* means?

_____

_____

_____

2 marks

14 Which of these could be a suitable title for the poem?

✓ Tick **one**.

Tummy rumbles ☐

Unending hunger ☐

Explain your choice.

This would make a good title because …

_____

_____

_____

2 marks

15 Read **Verse 7**.

What has the poet done at the end of each line?

Explain why he has used this effect.

_____

_____

_____

2 marks

From *Caribbean Carnival*

by Jillian Powell

Where in the world

The Caribbean islands lie in the Caribbean Sea to the east of Central America. Altogether, there are 7,000 islands, rocky islets, **coral reefs** and cays.

The islands have a warm, tropical **climate** with a dry season and a rainy season, and the risk of hurricanes from June to November. They have beautiful scenery including mountains and caves, rainforests and jungles, rolling hills, sugar cane fields and volcanoes. The white sandy beaches, warm seas and weather attract millions of tourists each year.

Carnival celebrations

In the Christian Catholic Church, people celebrated carnival on the days before Lent, the period of **fasting** leading up to Easter. These days, they're called Fat Sunday, Monday and Tuesday. Fatty foods, such as butter, eggs and meat, were eaten up until fasting began.

Carnival celebrations were introduced to the Caribbean by Europeans. Governors and **plantation** owners held grand **masquerade** parties, with costumes and masks, dancing, music and song.

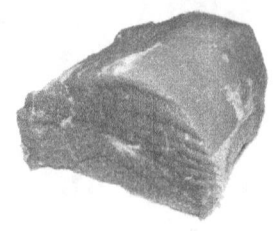

The word "carnival" means "putting away the meat".

When African slaves were freed from slavery by law in 1834, they adopted carnival to celebrate their freedom. It grew into a mix of European and African festivals, with colourful costumes, parades with dancing and music, contests and prizes. Carnival celebrates freedom, national feast days or the sugar cane harvest, as well as the last days before Lent.

Glossary	
climate	the type of weather in a particular area
coral reefs	sandy or rocky ridges in a tropical sea made of tiny coral skeletons
fasting	not eating food
masquerade	a party where everyone wears a mask
plantation	land (usually in a tropical area) where one crop is grown

From *The Story of Nian: A Folk Tale from China*
by Dr Wee Bee Geok

Chapter 1

Long ago in China, there was a terrible creature called Nian, which lived deep in the ocean. It had a huge body covered in spiky scales, and sharp horns on its long head. Its powerful pointed tail could shatter a boat with just one swoosh.

Nian didn't often come up from the water. But when it did, sailors shone their lights and blasted their horns to warn other ships and nearby villages about the creature. Only then did it quickly sink back into the sea. The fish nearby had to hide in the corals and reeds so that the monster didn't eat them in one gulp. Thankfully, for most of the time, Nian stayed at the bottom of the ocean.

Chapter 2

However, on the eve of every Chinese New Year, Nian clambered onto the shore and terrorised the villages. It attacked the village folk. It charged at the animals. It gobbled up the crops and destroyed whatever was in its path. Then it looked for other villages to attack. Everyone cried, "Run! Run!" as they heard its stomping footsteps approach.

People fled from the villages to the mountains to escape from the beast. When they returned after the monster had gone, they saw everything in ruins. Many of the houses were flattened. The grains in the barns were scattered all around and the crops in the farms were destroyed. The animals that the villagers had left behind were found killed or injured. It was a sad, sorry sight.

Year 3: Summer Test 2 – Answer booklet

| Name: | Class: | Date: |

Questions 1–8 are about *Caribbean Carnival* (pages 49–50).

1 Read the glossary. Choose **one** option to complete the sentence.

✓ Tick **one**.

A plantation is a piece of _____ .

land ☐   glossary ☐   coral ☐

1 mark

2 Read the section with the title ***Where in the world***.

Give **two** reasons people choose to go on holiday to the Caribbean.

1. _____

_____

2. _____

_____

2 marks

3 **Find** the word *cay* in the text. Which of these options is most likely to be the correct meaning.

✓ Tick **one**.

an iceberg ☐

a type of crocodile ☐

a small, sandy island ☐

a capital city ☐

1 mark

4 The text says that there is a *risk of hurricanes from June to November*.

Put ticks (✓) in the table to show which of these are **true** and which are **false**.

	True	False
Hurricanes happen every month.		
Hurricanes always happen in January.		
There is a possibility of hurricanes in November.		

1 mark

5 *Lent, the period of fasting*

What does the word *fasting* mean in this sentence?

_____

_____

1 mark

6 A carnivore is an animal that eats mainly meat.

Explain how the words *carnivore* and *carnival* are related.

_____

_____

_____

1 mark

7 **Find** and **copy** a word that describes the kind of party where everyone wears a mask.

_____

1 mark

8 *Carnival celebrates freedom*

Explain how this relates to the history of the Caribbean.

_____

_____

_____

2 marks

Questions 9–15 are about *The Story of Nian* (page 51).

9 Read the first paragraph. **Find** and **copy one** word that means *strong*.

_____

1 mark

10 *Thankfully, for most of the time, Nian stayed at the bottom of the ocean.*

Why does the writer use the word *Thankfully*?

✓ Tick **one**.

Nian is glad to be at the bottom of the ocean. ☐

Nian could not cause much harm under there. ☐

The fish could hide more easily. ☐

Sailors liked to use their lights. ☐

1 mark

11 Nian lives underwater most of the year.

Read the first paragraph of **Chapter 2**. Which word suggests Nian must have legs and feet?

_____

1 mark

12 **Find two** different ways the sailors announced danger.

1. _____

   _____

2. _____

   _____

2 marks

13 The word *sorry* is used in the last sentence of **Chapter 2**.

What is the meaning of the word 'sorry' in this sentence?

✓ Tick **one**.

miserable ☐

to apologise ☐

blamed ☐

not to do it again ☐

1 mark

14 Read the first paragraph of **Chapter 2**.

Find and **copy two** words that show how aggressive Nian could be.

1. _____

2. _____

2 marks

15 Imagine you are a villager returning from the mountains after New Year. How would you feel when you saw the village again? Give evidence from the text.

_____

_____

_____

_____

2 marks

Mark scheme for Autumn Half Term Test 1

Qu.	Content Domain	Requirement	Mark
		Mudpuddle Farm	
1	2b	**Award 1 mark** for Jigger.	1
2	2b	**Award 1 mark** for Diana and Mossop.	1
3	2g	**Award 1 mark** for reference to the fact that she asks questions but doesn't know any answers.	1
4	2d	**Award 1 mark** for old.	1
5	2c	**Award 1 mark** for all correct: 1 = Old Thunder entered the field. 2 = The dog noticed a smell. 3 = The animals slowly appeared from hiding. 4 = Diana wondered about Jigger's behaviour.	1
6	2e	**Award 1 mark** for Another creature is hiding in the field.	1
7	2a	**Award 1 mark** for answer that refers to the fact that the dog is moving quietly or carefully. **Award 1 mark** for saying that he is moving close to the ground, like a snake.	2
8	2d	**Award 1 mark** each for reference to: noise; cutting machinery.	2
		Letter to parents and carers	
9	2a	**Award 1 mark** for 2 correct answers: dangerous, injury.	1
10	2c	**Award 1 mark** for answer that indicates how she was at first (happy) and **1 mark** for what she thinks now (the activity is dangerous). Also accept that she now thinks the activity prevents learning.	2
11	2b	**Award 1 mark** for all 3 correct: Anya — built a tower Mr Shepherd — tried to get children back into class Class 3B — constructed a building like a castle.	1
12	2g	**Award 1 mark** for all 3 correct: She hopes the children get better at building – False. She hopes the parents and carers support her – True. She is writing to someone called Hope – False.	1
13	2a	**Award 1 mark** for very.	1
14	2b	**Award 1 mark** for reference to height, e.g. over a metre tall. **Award 1 mark** for reference to strength, e.g. strong enough for children to climb on it.	2
15	2a	**Award 2 marks** for 3 or 4 correct; **award 1 mark** for 2 correct: results — the final outcome replica — an exact copy retrieve — to find and bring back prevents — stops or blocks.	2
		TOTAL MARKS	20

Mark scheme for Autumn Half Term Test 2

Qu.	Content Domain	Requirement	Mark
		Spotlight on Brazil	
1	2b	**Award 1 mark** for 22 April 1500; also accept 1500.	1
2	2b	**Award 1 mark** for European settlers.	1
3	2a	**Award 1 mark** for all answers correct: appalling — terrible abolished — stopped fertile — good for growing settled — made a home.	1
4	2c	**Award 1 mark** for all answers correct: 1 = Native Indians lived in Brazil for thousands of years. 2 = Cabral first visited Brazil. 3 = Landowners discovered the land was fertile. 4 = Slaves were transported from Africa.	1
5	2g	**Award 1 mark** each for any two of the following: conditions on the ships; appalling treatment; early death (before age 30); being forced to work.	2
6	2a	**Award 1 mark** for rich.	1
7	2b	**Award 1 mark** for 2 correct answers; **award 2 marks** if all answers correct: Slaves were asked to make coffins – False. Pedro Álvares Cabral was travelling to India when he found Brazil – True. Landowners and slaves became very rich – False.	2
		Class Six and the Very Big Rabbit	
8	2b	**Award 1 mark** for reference to wiggling ears. Also accept reference to saying "I wish …".	1
9	2b	**Award 1 mark** for reading a book about rabbits.	1
10	2d	**Award 1 mark** each for any 2 from: same size; glasses; holding the same book.	2
11	2d	**Award 1 mark** for didn't want to hurt her feelings.	1
12	2d	**Award 1 mark** for any reasonable suggestion and **1 mark** for supporting evidence from the text, e.g. Confused – they didn't know how she had done it. Excited – they cheered.	2
13	2b	**Award 1 mark** for any of: she was Miss Bennett-sized; she had glasses like Miss Bennett; she was holding the book Miss Bennett had been reading.	1
14	2d	**Award 1 mark** for 2 correct answers; **award 2 marks** if all answers correct: The class had seen Miss Bennett turn into a rabbit before – False. Rachel was angry that Miss Bennett could not finish her story – False. The rabbit remained calm after the trick – True.	2
15	2g	**Award 1 mark** for surprise.	1
		TOTAL MARKS	**20**

Mark scheme for Spring Half Term Test 1

Qu.	Content Domain	Requirement	Mark
'I Invented the Frisbee'			
1	2b, 2d	**Award 1 mark** for on holiday.	1
2	2a	**Award 1 mark** for both correct answers: thin; lightweight.	1
3	2d	**Award 1 mark** for they were bored.	1
4	2g	**Award 1 mark** for zoom, dip, fly. Also accept spin.	1
5	2a	**Award 1 mark** for all answers correct: Frisbees and plates buzz and whirr – False. Frisbees don't make a sound as they fly – True. They whispered as they threw the plates – False.	1
6	2b	**Award 1 mark** for does.	1
7	2d	**Award 1 mark** for 3 correct; **award 2 marks** for all 4 correct: They didn't know anyone to tell about it – False. They were worried they would get in trouble – True. They forgot all about it – False. They knew it was wrong to throw plates – True.	2
8	2g	**Award 1 mark** for excitement.	1
*Fabulous Creatures – Are They Real?*			
9	2c	**Award 1 mark** for all answers correct: None of the creatures in the book exist – False. Myths and legends are types of stories – True. Fabulous creatures are from myths but not legends – False.	1
10	2b	**Award 1 mark** for feed him pieces of cake [soaked in honey].	1
11	2a	**Award 1 mark** for three heads and **1 mark** for dragon spines/spikes on his back.	2
12	2a, 2g	**Award 1 mark** for answers that refer to the creatures being unusual or having unusual features. **Award 2 marks** for a fully developed answer that explains the effect of surprise or wonder in the reader or refers to the creatures appearing in stories/myths/legends.	2
13	2b	**Award 1 mark** for all answers correct: fins – thick scales – heavy jaws – strong teeth – sharp.	1
14	2b	**Award 1 mark** for rock fossils and **1 mark** for fisherman found a live fish.	2
15	2b	**Award 1 mark** referring to it walking on strong fins. **Award 1 mark** for referring to it only walking underwater. **Award 2 marks** for an answer that explains the two different viewpoints or for an answer that takes a particular viewpoint and justifies it fully.	2
		TOTAL MARKS	20

Mark scheme for Spring Half Term Test 2

Qu.	Content Domain	Requirement	Mark
		**School Trip – Sam's Diary**	
1	2g	**Award 1 mark** for to show how it felt like a long time.	1
2	2a, 2b	**Award 1 mark** for dinner had been pizza / she didn't like pizza.	1
3	2b	**Award 1 mark** for 2 correct; **award 2 marks** for all 3 correct. Sam enjoyed sitting next to Faye – True. Faye moved after she had been sick – False. Sam hadn't really wanted to sit next to Faye – False.	2
4	2b	**Award 1 mark** for couldn't decide / kept changing her mind.	1
5	2b	**Award 1 mark** for do a handstand.	1
6	2a	**Award 1 mark** for 2–3 correct answers; **award 2 marks** for all 4 correct: portcullis – a defensive gate; artefact – an ancient or important object; broadsword – a weapon; curator – someone who works at a museum.	2
7	2b	**Award 1 mark** for 2–3 correct answers; **award 2 marks** for all 4 correct: Sam was told off by the curator – False. Billy had been sent home – True. The curator explained to the teacher to help Sam – True. The curator thought Sam was lucky to not go home – False.	1
8	2c	**Award 1 mark** for all answers correct: 1 = discussion about where to sleep 3 = talent contest 2 = dinner 4 = the trip to the castle.	1
		**Harry the Poisonous Centipede**	
9	2b	**Award 1 mark** for both correct answers: surprised, hurt.	1
10	2d	**Award 1 mark** for both correct answers: to prevent another creature harming him; to catch food to eat.	1
11	2a	**Award 1 mark** for silly.	1
12	2d	**Award 1 mark** for 2–3 correct answers; **award 2 marks** for all 4 correct: Harry's friend is called Belinda – False. Belinda is Harry's mother – True. Belinda lives in a hot climate – True. Harry lives in a different country to Belinda – False.	2
13	2d	**Award 1 mark** for difficulty pronouncing his name or speaking Centipedish. **Award 2 marks** where an answer develops the explanation further, e.g. by including the information about no vowels. Also allow 1 mark where an answer refers to the sound of the language being like crackling.	2
14	2c	**Award 1 mark** for an answer referring to both being in segments **Award 1 mark** for an answer referring to the cuticle; armoured covering; hard shiny dark stuff.	2
15	2c, 2d	**Award 1 mark** for option chosen that shows Harry was happy, and an explanation that includes phrases: thought it was fine or liked being what he was.	1
		TOTAL MARKS	20

Mark scheme for Summer Half Term Test 1

Qu.	Content Domain	Requirement	Mark
		Monster and Chips	
1	2d	**Award 1 mark** for all four lines drawn correctly: magic tokens — coins; stronghold — chip shop; quest — task; golden treasure — chips.	1
2	2a	**Award 1 mark** for perilous.	1
3	2a, 2g	**Award 1 mark** for an answer that indicates it showing Grace's meanness, or her character as a bully.	1
4	2b	**Award 1 mark** for all 3 correct: A dragon tried to eat Grace – False. Eating jelly made Grace angry – False. Joe was a type of duck – False.	1
5	2a	**Award 1 mark** for both correct answers: threatening and fierce.	1
6	2d	**Award 1 mark** for an answer referring to Grace's smelly breath.	1
7	2c	**Award 1 mark** for any of the following references: quest, magic tokens, Joe the Fearless, 'our hero', heroic daydream. Also accept: stronghold, monstrous horror if explained.	2
8	2b, 2d, 2e	**Award 1 mark** for predicting No. **Award 1 mark** for an any appropriate reference to the text, e.g. • He is going to trick Grace into moving away from the door. • He is going to think of a plan. Also accept reference to him remembering he is Joe the Fearless or a plausible suggestion for an action to outsmart Grace.	2
		'Hollow Legs'	
9	2g	**Award 1 mark** for teeth.	1
10	2a	**Award 1 mark** for any 2 from: crumb, bite, or chunk.	1
11	2d	**Award 1 mark** for an answer that shows the poet does not like broccoli and refers to evidence from the poem as the word 'unwanted' describes the broccoli spears.	1
12	2g	**Award 1 mark** for hearing.	1
13	2a	**Award up to 2 marks** for an answer that indicates the following properties: emptiness, darkness, depth, unknown area.	2
14	2c, 2d	**Award 2 marks** for an answer that is justified, e.g. [Tummy rumbles] would make a good title because ... the poet can never be full up, and the word rumble shows the noise an empty tummy makes. **Award 1 mark** for an answer which has some basic explanation, e.g. because it is about being hungry.	2
15	2b, 2g	**Award 1 mark** for noticing the repetition of the final word. **Award 1 mark** for recognising that the repetition is linked with the echoing sound in the verse.	2
		TOTAL MARKS	20

Mark scheme for Summer Half Term Test 2

Qu.	Content Domain	Requirement	Mark
		Caribbean Carnival	
1	2b	**Award 1 mark** for land.	1
2	2b	**Award 1 mark each** for any 2 from: sandy beaches; warm sea; warm weather; beautiful scenery.	2
3	2a	**Award 1 mark** for a small sandy island.	1
4	2a, 2d	**Award 1 mark** for all three correct. Hurricanes happen every month – False. Hurricanes always happen in January – False. There is a possibility of hurricanes in November – True.	1
5	2b	**Award 1 mark** for answer referring to going without food, or not eating for a time.	1
6	2a	**Award 1 mark** for an answer referring to the fact that both words have *carni-* in them meaning meat: *carnival* means to give up or 'put away' meat; *carnivore* means a person or animal that eats meat.	1
7	2b	**Award 1 mark** for masquerade. Accept minor spelling or copying errors.	1
8	2c	**Award 2 marks** for an answer that explains the freedom from slavery.	2
		The Story of Nian	
9	2a	**Award 1 mark** for *powerful*.	1
10	2g	**Award 1 mark** for Nian could not cause much harm under there.	1
11	2d	**Award 1 mark** for *clambered*. Also accept *charged*; *stomping*.	1
12	2b, 2d	**Award 1 mark** for using horns on their boats, and **1 mark** for shining or flashing lights from their boats.	2
13	2a	**Award 1 mark for** miserable.	1
14	2c	**Award up to 2 marks** for the following: *terrorised, attacked, charged, gobbled, destroyed, attack*. Also accept: *stomping*.	2
15	2e	**Award 2 marks** for a fully developed answer shows unhappiness and explains why – refers in detail to destruction. **Award 1 mark** that mentions only unhappiness or the destruction.	2
		TOTAL MARKS	**20**

Name: Class:

Year 3 Reading Comprehension Record Sheet

Tests	Mark	Total marks	Key skills to target
Autumn Half Term Test 1			
Autumn Half Term Test 2			
Spring Half Term Test 1			
Spring Half Term Test 2			
Summer Half Term Test 1			
Summer Half Term Test 2			

© HarperCollins*Publishers* Ltd 2019

www.ingramcontent.com/pod-product-compliance
Lightning Source LLC
Chambersburg PA
CBHW081436300426
44108CB00016BA/2383